Haseeb Administrative System

Mohannad Majid

MOHANNAD MAJID

Copyright © 2018 Mohannad Majid
All rights reserved.
ISBN: 9781728775234

Dedication

Firstly, I would like to dedicate this book to the Almighty God, the most observant and most merciful.

I wish to thank my parents who were my early teachers who led by way of example as a source of inspiration, guidance and love.

To my wife and daughters, much appreciation for their continues support in every way and for their patience, faith and partnership for the success of my life.

To all of my family members for their ultimately support and encourages.

I highly appreciate the efforts expended by my brother Mohammad and Dr. Saleh Sadiq for reviewing the Arabic edition of this book.

A special word of gratitude to my friend Brandon Brander for his extreme support during my stay in the U.A.E. and motivating me to translate my book from Arabic to English and for his assistance in editing this book..

Introduction

Like most people I was complaining and complaining about insufficient services in public offices, until I decided to contribute by finding a solution to real problems, and since there are no limits or restrictions that prevent my thinking, I went ahead.

I had searched for the causes of the problem between the employees and their duties. Particular questions came to mind.

Why do some employees fail in carrying out their jobs? Why is the salary equal to the employee who is dedicated to his work and another employee who is less committed?

Why is the performance of employees linked to their management? If a good manager controlled them, they do their duties successfully, but if the manager relaxes they consequently relax as well?

Why do great companies succeed in production and marketing while a lot of administrative plankton remains with the employee?

Why does an office employee, who receives hard transactions not have incentives like that of a salesperson or a factory worker? Does the office worker's task carry less value than them? Or the existence of an administrator is necessary to maintain the work performance? And if the office employee performs better, he might be rewarded.

What do we know about the integrity of the administration? How many good employees never received an incentive from the manager? How many bad employees stay because they know how to satisfy their manager? Some have a good relationship with the manager. They know exactly what he expects and what interests him. How many organizations have you visited whose employees are not punctual and who do not keep the working hours?

I decided to illicit and record such problems by interviewing staff and reading about it. I also consulted various reading material about diagnosing administrative corruption and staff treatment methods.

I jotted down ideas as it came to my mind. I searched for others who shared similar ideas. I was determined to spread the ideas in the hope that the problems might be solved in part or completely.

It wasn't important to apply the suggested system comprehensively, but in the spirit of applying it with the possibility of using it to suit the needs of all institutions.

Haseeb system is the suggested solution. With Haseeb system, the investment of staff time and the motivations to complete the transactions in quantity and quality, is greatly improved. Collaboration among staff, as members of one team, fights the idleness of employees and transaction delays, and limits negative courtesies at the expense of work. Through Haseeb system, staffs are rewarded for their good performance. It also encourages the acceleration of transactions and rotate staff between offices and sections of work. It reduces the stages of transaction completion, which in turn reflects the improved performance of the institution. The reform of any institution begins with the reform of every individual involved and attention to every transaction performed on site.

I hereby wish to thank all those employees who blocked my transactions, whether with good intentions or not; whether out of greed or just out of curiosity and interest; whether they delayed my transactions through their own misunderstanding or poor applications of carrying them out or not; whether these employees were just lazy or spiteful. Whatever the reasons were, this eventually inspired me to search for a solution seeking to transfer these anomalies away from such employees, so that the attention to transactions could be completely directed from the owner to the employee. Haseeb system was indeed that solution.

Mohannad Majid Saleem Al-Bosta
    17-9-2009

Contents

DEDICATION III
INTRODUCTION V
CHAPTER 1 DEFINITION OF HASEEB SYSTEM 9
  1.1 Introduction 9
  1.2 Structure of the Organization 10
  1.3 Classification of Departments and Institutions 11
  1.4 Principles of the Haseeb System 11
  1.5 The Idea of Haseeb System 13
    Example (1-1) 21
    Example (1-2) 28
  1.6 From One Office to Another 33
    Example (1-3) 34
    Example (1-4) 35
  1.7 Stages of a Treatment 38
    Example (1-5) 38
  1.8 The Department 39
    Example (1-6) 39
  1.9 Foundation 40
    Example (1-7) 41
  1.10 General Administration 41
    Example (1-8) 42
  1.11 Vital Sections 43
  1.12 Disbursement of the Financial Reward 44

CHAPTER 2   MECHANISM OF HASEEB SYSTEM FOR PAPER-WORK 45
2.1 Tools 45
2.2 Classification of Foundation Offices 47
1- Public Offices 47
2- Internal Offices 47
2.3 Mechanism of Dealing with Paper-Works 48
1- Outer Offices 48
2- Internal Offices 54
2.4 Haseeb Electronic System 56
2.5 Mainstreaming Haseeb System 56
REFERENCES 57

Chapter 1 Definition of Haseeb System

1.1 Introduction

Despite the efforts made by many Governments in fighting corruption, administrative diseases and employment slacks, it remained inherent to most government departments and institutions. Bribery and favoritism and favoring staff leaving, delaying or neglecting transactions and waiting for long-term reviewers between offices and lounges; all of them are real existing undeniable problems.

A lot of structural changes and corrections have been applied. Many laws and regulations proceeded. A lot of monitoring and inspection committees have been assigned; incentives and administrative controls were put in place. Despite all of this, corruption still exists, and if it was exposed on one side, it would still spread in other ways to take on new shapes and new labels.

The proposed administrative rule "Haseeb System" tries to manage and invest working time and removes many of the plankton of the administrations and transfers the interest towards the completion of the transaction from its owner to the staff. This causes the employee to be happy to receive the clients and the transactions.

The idea of this system was inspired by the incentives obtained in Islam, on Deeds. Sura Ar Rahman ayah 60 says: "Is the reward for anything but good?-   The Prophet Mohammad, -peace be upon him, said: "Whoever supplicates Allah to exalt my mention, Allah will exalt his mention ten times". And there is a requital for every single action whatever small or big. This should be the motivation the good Muslim seeks to do good deeds to increase his benefits and to erase his sins. The good word is a charity, and the smile in your brother's face is a charity. And so Islam encourages Muslims to care for all the work and behavior in his life, and rewards him quantitatively and qualitatively.

Administrative regulations have been introduced in factories and companies to motivate workers and sellers to develop their performance and increase their production and sales.

For example, factories determine the number of produced units that a worker should prepare during a specific time, and if he produces more he gets more incentives. Companies also specify targets for salesman and if he sells more he gets more bonuses.

The idea of such a proposed system would require that employees be given incentives for their performance for each transaction quantitatively and qualitatively. Incentives and bonuses meet the needs of the human soul. This makes the staff member feel satisfied and acknowledged according to his work and performance, as well as his feeling of the spirit of justice and increases his loyalty and affiliation to his institution. It also raises the spirit of cooperation and solidarity. The idea of such a system was therefore based on giving incentives in the form of performance points for each transaction going through the staff member and the office. The more the staff member uses his or her time to perform more transactions, the more points are made. And because the money is the strongest stimuli, a financial reward can be paid for the number of points earned by a staff member during his or her work hours.

The reason for the giving of the name of "Haseeb" on this system is its ability to account and follow every employee and every transaction however small or large. So, I used the (Arabic word) Haseeb formula for an artistic weight, which is a sign of over accounting and follow-up. It is often used in a way which indicates that a person is a specialist in accounting and control.

To introduce the Haseeb system, we must first start with definitions specified to this system which help us understand it more accurately.

1.2 Structure[1] of the Organization

The organization which aims to apply Haseeb system is to be sectionalized to:

- Main Office: The office of the general-director of the foundation.

---

[1] The used structure here may vary for different states, countries and even from one organization to another.

- Department: Any administrative grouping performs certain functions, and one department consists of an office or a group of offices.
- Office: It has a function or specialized functions; each office is to be run by a staff member or group of staff members who deploy specific duties.

While staff members are classified to the:
- Institution manager: It is intended for the general director of the foundation.
- Department manager: a manager of the department.
- Office manager: He is the chief officer of an office.
- Permanent employee: is the employee who works permanently in an office.
- Visitor employee: If transactions are accumulated in an office through one of the working periods, the office can hire staff from other offices which are less busy. These staff members are called visitors.

1.3 Classification of Departments and Institutions

Departments and institutions are classified based on dealing with transactions to:
1. Institutions which deal with paperwork.
2. Institutions use paperwork and at the same time receive transactions electronically.
3. Institutions that deal only with electronic transactions.
4. Organizations dependent on the presence of clients like hospitals.

1.4 Principles of the Haseeb System

Incentives and sanctions of the Haseeb system is similar to those adopted in many factories, where workers are required to assemble or produce their targets during the working time. If more pieces were produced within the working time, an additional incentive will be given to the workers, and vice versa. Also, if the piece was produced by a number of stages they are distributed by the so-called production line, so, the line working members are treated according to their performance as a team.

If we look at the production line members of the factory, we find them developing their skills and their cooperation to accomplish the greatest number of pieces and to accumulate more money. The absentee does not receive incentives for the pieces made by his colleagues who are present. Thus, the existing workers are rewarded according to their performance and diligence. This method modifies workers equality and motivation. With fairness, motivation, encouragement and a sense of belonging, factories have succeeded and developed.

The Haseeb system considers each office as a production line, and the office staffs are considered to be as the members of the production line. If the employees collaborate as members of one team in the production line, their performance is going to be improved and developed. Cooperation is vital!

If an employee can be relied upon more than his colleagues, then he will provoke resentment because of the lack of fairness in the work place. This is almost due to the unequal distribution of the duties, and because of the leisure time of an employee more than others, or because of continuous absence of a staff member will force his colleagues to take on added duties without compensation. All the said phenomenon is considered to destroy the sense of equality amongst employees which the suggested Haseeb system fights against and limits.

Also, the Haseeb system tracks the transaction, no matter how small or large it is, from one office to another and from one department to another until it is completed. In addition, the system judges those defaulting on transactions, and at the same time, rewards the optimist. It is easy for managers to track the activities and work of offices and employees without depicting any favoritism or embarrassment using the Haseeb system which in turn can contribute to possible and probable promotion decisions.

1.5 The Idea of Haseeb System

Working Periods: If the working day starts (for example) with the presence of staff at 8^{30} AM until 5^{30} PM, then the Haseeb system requires the institution to divide the working day into equal periods. For example, if the working day is divided into four periods, the first one should start at 9^{00} AM until 11^{00} AM, and so on until the fourth period which starts at 3^{00} until 5^{00} PM

The Haseeb System Committee: The organization must form a committee to study and classify transactions, and to monitor and develop the system to adapt to the changing environment and renewable services of the foundation.

Classification of Transactions: Not all papers received for an office are considered transactions. Various transactions cannot be equated in terms of the number of required documents, acting steps and the taken actions. Here comes the role of the Haseeb system committee in defining transactions, specifying the beginning and end for each transaction through the offices, in addition to classification of transactions into categories by required time to complete and review the transaction at each office. Suppose for example, a transaction consisting of one paper and needs an officer to complete review, audit, comment on it and make the related decision within one minute, so, this can be classified to fall in transaction of first category in this office.

Transaction Category: It is the category rated according to the standard period of completing the transaction, taking into account the number of papers and the requirements of the transaction for documenting, auditing and making decisions about it.

Standard Time of Completing a Transaction (ST): It is the average time required to complete a transaction by one officer. Each category of the transaction has its own standard time (**ST**) depending on the receiving office and the taken actions taken during this period. The standard time is measured in minutes. It can be changed to seconds as the committee deems fit according to the operational requirements of the enterprise.

The Haseeb system gives an additional timeout for completing one transaction called **Grace Time for One Transaction (GT)**. My suggestion is that **Grace Time** should double the standard time, whereby each organization can decide its own grace time.

The following formula shows this relationship as:

Grace Time for One Transaction (GT) equals to double the standard of treatment.

$$GT = 2\ ST \qquad (1)$$

Upon arrival **a Packet of Transactions** to an office (which is many transactions of different categories delivered together to an office), so, the **Standard Time to Complete a Packet of Transactions (SP)** is equal to the sum of the multiplications of the standard time of completing a transaction (**ST**) and the frequency of each category (**f**) divided by **Number of Permanent Employees in the Office (NE)**. Henceforth, an office with two permanent employees cannot be equated with another office with many employees and both are serving the same packet of transactions.

$$SP = \frac{\sum_{TC} ST_{TC} \times f_{TC}}{NE} \qquad (2)$$

Grace Time for One Packet (GP): is twice of standard time for completing a packet of transactions (**SP**). Each organization can change the value to suit its needs. Here the Grace Time for One Packet (**GP**) shouldn't exceed a working period, otherwise, the office manager must ask for visitor employee/s from other offices to complete the task before the end of the period, Haseeb system can predict in advance the office's need for staff and inform the office manager to take the necessary precautions.

$$GP = 2 \times SP \qquad (3)$$

When the office completes all or some of the transactions of the package, so the **Action Time (AT)** is the time spent by the office in completing one transaction from the packet, starting from beginning of the next working period until delivery time to the next office.

$$AT = \text{delivery time of the transaction} - \text{starting of the next working period} \quad (4)$$

And here, the working period is the first following period after the delivery of the packet to the office, and we will discuss it in details in the working mechanism.

If some transactions from the packet remain without competition, so the **Remaining Time (RT)** can be defined as the summation of standard times of completing remaining transactions, which wasn't completed by the office of the same packet.

$$RT = \frac{\sum_R ST_R \times f_R}{NE} \quad (5)$$

Where **(R)** symbolizes the remaining transactions.

Each transaction has a multiplying factor **(A)** through the following relationship:

$$A = 2 - \frac{AT}{|SP - RT|} \quad (6)$$

The properties of this factor will be described in the coming examples. The introduced number 2 is due to the suggested ratio between the grace time (**GT**) and the standard time of completing a transaction (**ST**) in equation (1), and the fraction is the ratio between action time (**AT**) and the absolute value of the difference between standard time to complete a packet of transactions (**SP**) and the remaining time (**RT**).

If the entire transaction packet is completed with less time than the standard, the factor **A** becomes positive, and vice versa. and it will be explained in the examples (1-1) and (1-2). Also, the Standard Multiplying Factor A_s equals one when the action time (**AT**) is equal to the standard time for completing a transaction packet (**SP**).

Thus, when a transaction packet arrives, the office is going to complete and deliver it as soon as possible without delay, because the Haseeb system counts the working time for each transaction and the longer the office delays, the more negative factor **A** becomes for each late transaction.

The A factor for each transaction is allowed to reach a negative critical value, **Alarm Coefficient (M),** which is determined by the committee. The alarm coefficient **M** helps to judge the treatment of each transaction as:

A > M	Treatment in good /acceptable mode.
A = M	The treatment is late, and an instant attention is to be directed to the office manager notifying him about the late treatment.
A < M	The treatment is too late, and a warning is given to the office manager and notifying that the transaction must be completed immediately. Add to that, the factor **A** becomes negative, which is not in the interest of the office members.

We note that the Haseeb system is giving penalties to the office manager more than other staff, because he represents the office and carries the responsibility for organizing his office and staff aiming to get high performance level.

At the end of each period, the Haseeb system collects **Office Points during a Period (PP)** which equals to the sum of the product of each transaction category **TC** (completed or still in progress during the period) and its **A** factor:

$$PP = \sum_{i=1}^{N} TC_i \times A_i \qquad (7)$$

Where **N** is the total number of transactions completed or still in progress in the office during the working period.

And here the **A** factor to be counted continuously and cumulatively for late treatment each period every day until the office has completed and delivered it into the following office, only then, the cumulative attrition of the factor **A** stops.

The office manager harvests office points for a period (**PM**) which equals to the Ratio[2] of manager points (**R**) times the office points in from the period (**PP**)

$$PM = R \times PP \qquad (8)$$

Add to that, the manager gets Points of Employee (**PE**) as other employees in the office who are present during the period

$$PE = \frac{(1 - R) \times PP}{NE_p + VE_p} \qquad (9)$$

where **NE_p is the Number of Office Employees present during the period** including the manager of the Office, **VE_p: Number of visitor employees during the period.**

Monitor the presence of employee: Every employee places a card in a monitor device to prove his presence, and here the manager and the employees will be careful not to falsify this because the presence of a card that is not present will be at their expense or generosity. Employee presence is monitored electronically by a reader placed on the room entrance or a reader within the office where the employee places his or her card while he or she is in the service. Also, the employee presence might be monitored by the manager who registers the presence of each employee.

To monitor the performance of the Office; at the end of each fiscal month, the **Total Monthly Points for the Office (TM)** is the total summation of office points (**PP_m**) during all the counted fiscal monthly periods.

---

[2] The Ratio of manager points (R) is identified by the committee.

$$TM = \sum_{m=1}^{month} PP_m \qquad (10)$$

m=1,2,... number of month periods

The more **TM** achievements indicates the more office performance.

Each employee in the organization has **Employee Monthly Points (ME)** which is the total number of employee points for all month periods:

$$ME = \sum_{m=1}^{month} PE_m \qquad (11)$$

And in the same way, the manager of the office has **Managers Monthly Points (MM)**. They are the sum of the director's points during Periods Month and earned from its percentage in the office plus its points as an employee.

$$MM = \sum_{m=1}^{month} PM_m + \sum_{m=1}^{month} PE_m \qquad (12)$$

Thus, the performance of the manager and employee can be evaluated at any time of the month. Consequently, a **Financial Bonus (FB)** can be added to the monthly salary and is equal to the **Financial Value for the Point (B)** times the total number of monthly points.

$$FB = B \times Monthly\ Points \qquad (13)$$

Note the following:
- The Haseeb system motivates the office employee to work maximally within a good team spirit, as the failure of one affects everyone.
- It stimulates the office manager to properly allocate tasks to its staff and immediately substitute the absentee or rescue visitor employees

when needed; delaying or error treatment has a high price for all, and the speed of achievement is rewarded.
- The staff will be quick to collect transactions to earn more time before the start of the next working period to increase the value of the factor **A**.
- Also, staff will be pleased to increase the number of transactions received to their office because more transactions lead to more points.
- The system pushes the institution manager to improve the staff levels; reduces inefficient employee services and replaces them with the most active and efficient employee. There is no place in the Haseeb system except for active members.
- No transaction will be delayed because the employee does not exist, the Haseeb system punishes managers and staff for the delays and must find a replacement for the missing staff member.
- There will be no assigned work to a staff member more than another, all of whom must cooperate by working hard as members of the same team, because they are all involved in the reward or retribution.
- This system will limit phenomena such as the out-of-office and out-of-institution at working times; the lack of presence during transactions packet means that they are denied additional points.
- Limits negative courtesies, the director or staff of the office will not consider the absence or outgoing employee as attendance during work, as this will reduce their share of points or it will be considered a generosity to them.
- The office members can predict the coming transactions in the next periods and adjust themselves. If there are accumulated transactions, everyone will seriously work on completing them. They may ask for help from visitor employees. On the other hand, if there are few transactions, the employee can go and help staff who are under pressure in other office, and collect additional points, or that employee may get permission to leave when necessary.
- The Haseeb system fights delays of any transaction no matter what it is. The presence of the **A** factor which causes attention or warning to the office in case A becomes equal or less than the alarm coefficient

M, due to the delay of a transaction. This negative indicator is not wanted by the office manager or staff, especially as it affects the assessment of points, performance, promotions and rewards.

All the above can be understood during the following examples. As mentioned previously, the value of the grace time and the financial value of the point, as well as the alarming coefficient and the ratio of manager points differ according to the institution's needs.

Example (1-1)

Assume an organization uses Haseeb system, and the working day[3] starts at 8^{00} AM, and ends at 5^{00} PM. The working day is divided into four working periods, two hours for each. The first period starts at 9^{00} AM, and so on. The financial value for one point, **B**, equals to 0.5 $. The alarm coefficient, **M**, equals -18 and 6 staff members including the manager work in an office. The ratio of manager points **R**= 0.2. At the end of a Thursday working day, the office received a transactions packet of various categories according to the following table:

Table 1

Transaction category TC	Frequency f	Standard time of completing the transaction ST	Grace time for a transaction GT
1	38	1	2
2	35	2	4
3	20	3	6

So, the standard time to complete the transactions packet
SP= (38 × 1 + 35 × 2 + 20 ×3) /6 = 28 minutes
Grace time for the packet
GP= 56 minutes

To simplify and clarify the idea, we assume that no other transactions packet was received by the office on the next Saturday and Sunday.

Note: Since the transaction was received at the end of a Thursday, the working period will be counted from the first following period on Saturday at 9^{00} AM.

Now there are several possibilities and we will discuss some of them:

---

[3] When the book was written in Libya in 2008, the working days were Saturday- Thursday

First Case

The staff of the Office starts working on the packet immediately and completes it before they leave on Thursday, and then, to deliver it on Saturday morning after it is presented, at 8^{45} AM. Then:

Remaining time = **RT**= 0, where all packet transactions were completed.

Number of office employees =**NE**= 6

Number of office employees at the period= **NE**$_p$ = 6, where everyone was working during the period.

VE$_p$= Zero, where no visitor employee was there.

Action time = **AT**= 8^{45}-9^{00} = -15 minutes, and note that the working time is negative because the delivery time is preceded by the next working period.

Multiplying **A** factor per transaction =**A**=2-[(-15)/28]= 2.54

So, the office points during the period gained from this transactions packet

PP = 2.54 × (38 × 1 + 35 × 2 + 20 × 3) = 426.72 points. The points were distributed as follows:

Points of each employee from the period = **PE** = 56.896

Points of the office manager from the period= **PM** = 85.344 in addition to his points as a member of the office.

And so the employee's reward from this Period=28.448 $

The manager is rewarded = 42.672 + 28.448 = 71.12 $

A good reward was granted to the staff because of their diligence and initiative to work, and not to leave work for the next day.

Second Case

The office staffs opened the packet at 9^{00} AM on Saturday and completed all and delivered it at 9^{30} AM, exceeding the standard time to complete the packet (**SP**) by two minutes, so:

Remaining time, **RT**= 0, where all packet transactions were completed.

Action time = **AT**= 9^{30}-9^{00} =30 minutes.

Multiplying **A** factor per transaction = **A**=2 - [30/28] =0.93

So the office points outcome from this transactions pack = 0.93x (38 × 1 + 35 × 2 + 20 × 3) = 156.24 points; to be distributed as follows:

Employee points of the period = **PE** = 20.832

Manager points of the period = **PM** = 31.248, plus points as a member of the office.

So, the employee's reward from this period= 10.416 $, and the manager is rewarded = 15.624 + 10.416 = 26.04 $.

Employees have also been rewarded for accomplishing their work with less than the allowed grace time, but of course their bonuses are less than in the first case, as the Haseeb system rewards all according to diligence.

Third Case

The office staffs opens the packet at 9^{00} AM, completed and delivered them at 9^{56} AM, after the grace time of. Then:

Remaining time= **RT**= 0, where they completed all packet transactions.

Action time = **AT**= 9^{56} -9^{00} = 56 minutes.

Multiplying **A** factor per transaction =**A** = 2-[56/28]=0

Here, Haseeb system does not grant any reward for the office members from this transactions package, since they have not invest their time as the best to complete these packet. The standard time to complete the packet is 28 min which was evaluated by the committee to be more than the real needed time to fulfill it. The manager and staff must rearrange and organize themselves to increase their efficiency and points.

Fourth Case

The officers opened the transactions packet at 9^{30} AM, Saturday and finished all of them and delivered at 12^{00} PM. Then:

The action time is starting from the beginning of the period 9^{00}, regardless of the office's delay in receiving or opening the packet, thus:

Remaining time= **RT**= 0, where all packet transactions were completed.

Action time = **AT**= 12^{00}-9^{00} = 180 minutes. We note that the delay has been more than six times the grace time.

Multiplying **A** factor for each transaction

=**A**=2-[180/28]=-4.43, here the **A** factor is negative, because of the delay.

The points of the office from this transactions pack

=**PP**= -4.43x (38 × 1 + 35 × 2 + 20 × 3) = -744 point; to be distributed as follows:

Points of the employee = **PE** =-99.2 points

Points of the manager= **PM** =-148.8 points, plus points as a member of the office.

And so, the deducted amount from every employee because of delaying this transaction packet is 49.6 $.

The total deducted amount from manager is 124 $

Note that the opponent amount on the manager is more because he is the responsible of organizing his office. He has the lion's share of the bonus in the first and second cases because of the good performance under his management; and so in the case of deficient office performance, he's going to get the biggest share of the opponent. And he and his staff must reorganize themselves. And maybe they now find a motivation to improve their performance in future transaction packets until they compensate for their loss.

Haseeb system fights delaying of task accomplishment and work-leave. Only the employee who is concerned about his hard work can stay and benefit and they who are lazy and less concerned must leave and find another job.

Delays in transactions due to the absence of one staff will come up with consequences for him and his colleagues, since then, he won't get extra points, and it will affect the performance of the office. Haseeb system forces all members to deal with each other as members in one team so that they could perform their tasks best.

Fifth Case

The office opens the transaction packet at 9^{00} AM, Saturday, and completed the transactions of categories 1 and 2 and delivered to the next office at 9^{10} AM, while category 3 transactions were accomplished and delivered at 9^{15} AM of the next day (Sunday). Then:

In the first period of Saturday:
Transactions that are not completed from the same packet:

20 transactions of category 3, with standard time per transaction: **ST**= 3 minutes, thus:

Remaining time = **RT**= 3 × 20 / 6 = 10 minutes.

And so, at the end of the first period in Saturday, the action time for the unfinished remaining transactions = 120 minutes:

$A_{unfinished}$= 2-[120÷|28-10|] =-4.66

Office points from uncompleted transactions

$PP_{uncompleted}$ =-4.66x (20 × 3) =-280 points.

Transactions completed of this package:

Action time = 9^{10}-9^{00} = 10 minutes. Which is the time of transaction completion of categories 1 and 2.

$A_{accomplished}$= 2-[10÷|28-10|] = 1.44

Office points from Completed transactions

$PP_{completed}$= 1.44x (38 × 1 + 35 × 20) = 155.52 point

Office points from this package in the first period of Saturday =-280 + 155.52 =-124.48 points.

Second, third and fourth periods of Saturday:

And here as we mentioned, 20 transactions of the third category of the package weren't completed during any of Saturday's periods:

The second period: 11^{00} AM to 1^{00} PM

Action time for uncompleted transactions = 1^{00} -9^{00} = 240 minutes.

$A_{uncompleted}$= 2-[240÷|28-10|] =- 11.33

And the new **A** factor will replace the previous **A** factor in the first period, because it belongs to the same transactions.

Office points from the uncompleted transactions

PP =-11.33 (20 × 3) =-679.99 points

And consequently, the situation in repeated for the following periods; and in the end of the fourth Saturday period:

Action time for uncompleted transactions = 5^{00} -9^{00} = 480 minutes

Multiplying **A** factor

$A_{uncompleted}$= 2-[480÷|28-10|] =-24.66

which replaces the calculated **A** factor in the third period, and so on.

Office points from uncompleted transactions

PP =-24.66x (20 × 3) =-1480 points

Total office points from Saturday periods= 155.52 + (-1480) =-1324.48 points

Note: $A_{uncompleted}$ factor was continuously decreasing. At the beginning of the fourth hour (3^{00} PM) the value of $A_{uncompleted}$ factor reached -18 which equals the alarm coefficient **M**, whereupon, an attention will be directed (through the Haseeb system) to the office to expedite delivery of delayed transactions. As the time passed, the $A_{uncompleted}$ factor becomes less than **M=-18**, and a warning is recorded for the office at the end of the fourth period.

On the following Sunday, the office finished and delivered these transactions at 9^{15}AM, and here:

Action time=**AT**= 9^{15}-9^{00} + (480) = 495 minutes

Remaining time = **RT**= 0, where all transactions of this package were delivered

A factor= **A**= 2- [495÷28] =-15.68

and replace the previous **A** factor for the same transactions.

The office points from these transactions after its delivery on Sunday = -15.68 × (20 × 3) =-940.71 points

So, the total office points from this transaction packet

= -940.71+155.52= -785.19 points

The deduction amount from the office due to delays in these transactions = 392.597 $

52.346 $ was deducted from each employee.

And the deducted amount from the manager = 78.519 + 52.346 = 130.866 $.

If we assume that only one transaction has been delayed, the multiplying **A** factor is going to be less than the alarm coefficient **M**, which sends an attention to the office manager and he must find this transaction and accomplish it.

The manager must prove his administrative efficiency, if he led the office for better, his rewards will be generous, otherwise his share of the penalty would be more, and the less points he gains, the chance of staying as an office manager is less.

Also, if the office has a lot of staff members with few duties, its points will be divided by the large number of them, which leads to lower their rewards, and hence, some of them will ask for moving to another office to get more work and more points.

The financial incentives provided by the Haseeb system will help in improving the conditions of an active employee and ending the phenomenon of relaxing lazy employee. Lazy employee has no rewards in Haseeb system, and he will improve his performance or leave the place for better ones.

Haseeb system will create a different community of staff, a community works as a team, loves to work, takes some in the other's hands.

When a new employee arrives to the office; his colleagues will carry out improving his performance. Especially in the trial period, his performance will reflect the available cooperation in the office.

Example (1-2)

Ahmad, Mohammad, Adel and Saeed work under management of Asaad in an office followed the same institution mentioned in the example (1-1). At the end of Thursday, the office was informed that their office will receive a packet of 350 transactions in the first working period of Saturday, while in the second period another packet of 100 transactions will be delivered to the office according to the following table:

Table 2

Category (TC)	Standard time of completing one transaction (ST) min.	Grace time for one transaction (GT) min.	Saturday	
			First period Frequency (f)	Second period Frequency (f)
1	1	2	210	50
2	2	4	75	19
3	3	6	30	15
4	4	8	25	16
	Standard time for the packet (SP) in minutes		550/5 = 110	197/5 = 39.4
	Standard time for the packet (GP) in minutes		220	78.8

First Case

Note that the grace time[4] of the first packet is greater than the first period; then the manager of the office must- by the help of Haseeb system- call visitor employees from less busy offices to help. Also, the manager of the Office also assured his staff that they should be present on Saturday.

First Saturday's period: two visitor employees, Salem and Amer

---

[4] Here we recall that the action time is the sum of standard times for packet transactions divided by the number of permanent office staff **NE**.

(from another offices), joined the office to complete all packet transactions and delivered at 10^{50} AM:

Remaining time for this package =**RT**= 0, where they completed all the transactions.

Action time=**AT** = $10^{50} - 9^{00}$ = 110 minutes.

Number of employees = number of permanent employees of the office who was in the period + Visitors = **NE+VE**= 5 + 2 = 7

The multiplying factor **A** for the transaction = **A**= 2-[110÷|110-0|] = 1

Office points of the period = 1 × 550 = 550 points

Points for every employee including visitors = 78.57 points

Points of the office manager = 110 + 78.57 = 188.57 points

After the work is done in the period the visitor employees can go back to their offices.

Second Saturday's period: The grace time for the incoming transaction package is about 79 minutes, which is less than the duration of the period, then the staff of the office can accomplish it effortlessly and the manager can send any of his staff to assist as a visitor employee in any other office with stacked transactions. For example, Ahmad was sent as a visitor to another office.

The four employees received the second transactions pack at the beginning of the second period, completed it and delivered it at 12^{05} PM, then:

Remaining time for this package, **RT**= 0, where they completed all the transactions.

Action time = $12^{05} - 11^{00}$ = 65 minutes

Number of employees = number of permanent employees of the office who was in the period + Visitors=**NE+VE** = 4 + 0 = 4

The multiplying **A** factor for a transaction =**A** = 2-[65÷|39.4-0|] = 0.35

Office points of the second period = 0.35 x 197 = 69 points

Points for each employee except Ahmed = 17.25 points

Points of the office manager = 13.8 + 17.25 = 31.05 points

No points were added (from this packet) to Ahmad because he

wasn't existed, but he is going to gain points of being helping another office.

Final outcome

Office points from both periods = 550 + 69 = 619

Permanent employee points (Except Ahmed) of the two periods= 78.57 + 17.25 = 95.82 points.

The manager points of both periods = 188.57 + 31.05 = 257.57 points.

Salem and Amer benefited from the help of this office by 78.57 points.

For Ahmad, in addition to the 78.57 points which he gained in the first period, he increased his points by going as a visitor to another office.

The non-use of visitor staff will delay the completion of the first transaction packet to the second period; and consequently, the work is accumulated, and the delivery is delayed at the expense of the points.

Second Case

The manager of the office assured his staff of the need to be present on Saturday; he did not agree to call any visitor employee.

Saturday's first period: The office employees completed the packet's transactions of categories 1 and 2 during the first period and delivered it at 10^{45} AM, then:

Remaining time for this package, **RT**= (90+100)//5 = 38 minutes, where transactions of categories 3 and 4 were uncompleted.

Action time = $10^{45} - 9^{00}$ = 105 minutes.

Number of staff = number of permanent office staff present during the period + Visitors =**NE**+**VE**= 5 + 0 =5

Multiplying **A** factor for completed transactions = $A_{completed}$ = 2- [105÷|110-38|] = 0.54

Office points from completed transactions in the first period= 0.54 × (210+150) = 194.4 points

At the end of the period, Haseeb system recorded uncompleted transactions from categories 3 and 4.

Action time for uncompleted transactions $= 11^{00} - 9^{00} = 120$ minutes.

Multiplying **A** factor for uncompleted transactions $= \mathbf{A}_{uncompleted} = 2 - [120 \div |110-38|] = 0.33$

Office points from the unfinished transactions in the first period $= 0.33 \times 190 = 62.7$ points

Saturday's second period: The employees received the second packet; an extra work was added to the remaining uncompleted transactions from the first packet.

Each package is treated separately and let us assume the staff had completed the remaining transactions of the first packet and delivered it at 12^{00} PM.

The remaining time for the first packet coefficients $= 0$; The first packet was delivered completely.

Action time $= 12^{00} - 9^{00} = 180$ min

The multiplying **A** factor for transactions in categories 3 and 4 of the first packet after delivery $= \mathbf{A} = 2-[180 \div |110-0|] = 0.36$, which replaced the previous **A** factor for the same transactions and calculated at the end of the first period (0.33).

Office points from categories 3 and 4 of the first packet after delivery $= 69.09$, and replace the points for the same transactions which calculated at the end of the first period (62.7).

The transactions of categories 1, 2 and 3 of the second packet were also completed and delivered at 1^{00} PM, at the end of the second period, and hence:

The remaining time of uncompleted transactions of category 4 from the second packet $= 12.8$ minutes.

Action time $= 1^{00} - 11^{20} = 120$ minutes.

The multiplying **A** factor for the completed transactions of the second packet $= \mathbf{A}_{completed} = 2-(120 \div |78.8-12.8|) = 0.18$

Office points from completed transactions from the second packet $= 0.18 \times 133 = 24.18$ points.

At the end of the second period, as the office did not deliver transactions of category 4 for the second package:

Multiplying **A** factor for uncompleted transactions (category 4) of the second packet = $A_{uncompleted}$ = 2-[120 / |78.8-12.8|] = 0.18

Office points from category 4 = 0.18 × 64 = 11.64

Saturday's third period:

Finally, the office completed remaining transactions of the second packet and delivered it at 1^{25} PM, so:

The remaining time of the second packet = **RT** = 0

Action time = 1^{25} - 11^{00} = 145 minutes

The multiplying **A** factor for transactions of category 4 from the second package after delivery = **A** = 2- [145÷|78.8-0|] = 0.16 and replace the calculated factor at the end of the previous second period (0.18).

Office points from transactions of category 4 of the second packet after delivery = 0.16× 64 = 10.23, and replace the calculated points at the end of the second period (11.64 points).

The final outcome:

Total office points from the first and second packages during the three periods = 194.4 + 69.09 + 24.18 + 10.23 = 297.9 points

Points per employee = 47.64 points

Office manager's points = 59.58 + 47.64 = 107.22 Point

Transactions were delivered much longer than in the first case and the office staffs were awarded lower points.

In the first case, the transactions were delivered in an ideal time and the office and the staff members reaped more points, and they had more free time so that Ahmad was gone as a visitor employee to harvest more points.

Thus, Haseeb system encourages the acceleration of transactions and the rotation of staff between offices and departments, and contributes to correct and evaluate the performance of offices and staff, as well as the follow-up of each transaction, office and staff.

1.6 From One Office to Another

Haseeb system is not limited to tracking transactions in one office, because procedures for any transaction may be completed through many offices. And if two offices are going to treat the same transaction in different stages and steps, they may differ in terms of the transaction category and standard time for completing the taken actions and decisions. For example, office 11 is to scrutinize four statements for transaction number 519 and explain on it then transfer it into the following office number 13 which checks a single statement and issues an order for approval or rejection. Therefore, when establishing Haseeb system in the organization, all procedures for all transactions should be emulated in different offices, and then the standard transaction time for each transaction in each office can be specified. And in the said example, the transaction 519 may classified into category 4 at office 11 but it is classified into category 1 at the next office 13, and so on.

Also, office 11 may do mistakes in treating a transaction and then transfer it into office 13. If office 13 discovered the error, it should return it to the previous responsible office 11 and send a copy to inform the office of the referee.

The function of the referee office (Which consists of an employee or committee of staff) is concerning in reviewing, checking and errors verification according to allegation of an office about transferred transactions to it with mistakes, which would entail the return of the transaction to the source, and consequently delays the treatment.

Example (1-3)

Let's study some cases of office 13's claiming about incoming mistaken transaction from office 11, and the judges that may be made by the referee office

a) If the office 13's claim was true, then the transaction is considered completed for the office 13 in addition to bonus points equated the total standard points of the office 11 for the same transaction. The standard points of transaction/s (**ST**) in an office are

$$ST = \sum_i A_{standard,i} \times TC_i \qquad (14)$$

In this example, the transaction standard points, **ST**(office11, **CT**=4) = 1 × 4 = 4, where $A_{standard}=1$, **CT**= 4.

The multiplying **A** factor for office 11 from this returned transaction varies according to:

$$A_{\text{returned for mistake}} = \begin{cases} \text{zero}, & A_{\text{previous value}} > \text{zero} \\ -|A_{standard}|, & A_{\text{previous value}} = \text{zero} \\ -2|A_{\text{previous value}}|, & A_{\text{previous value}} < \text{zero} \end{cases} \qquad (15)$$

Also, the standard points that office 13 had gained from this transaction will be subtracted from office 11. And then, office 11 begins to deal with the same transaction as a new one.

b) If what office 13 alleged was wrong, the multiplying **A** factor that he got from his accomplishment of the transaction is subjected to equation (15) and the transaction is returned to office 13 to deal with again. The office 11 acquires the standard points for treatment by office 13, which in turn are deducted from it; and so on.

In both cases the referee office is governed by Haseeb system and must make the decision on the complaint within the specified time, and the delay will also make his points negative.

Example (1-4)

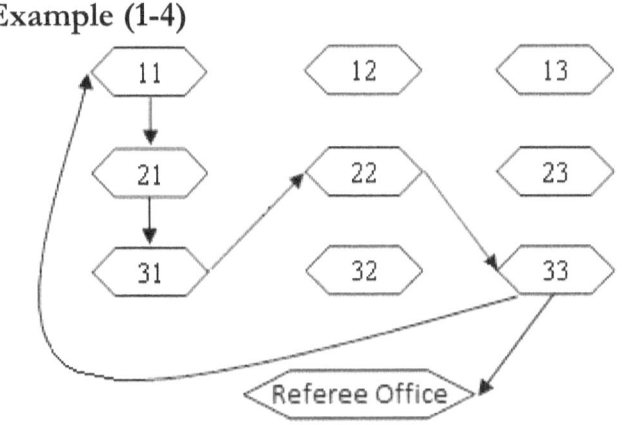

Figure 1: The treatment progress of a mistaken transaction form 519

The chart in Figure 1 shows the treatment progress of a transaction form 519 from office 11 to finally reach the office 33. The office 33 claimed errors in the performance of office 11 and sent it back to it and sent a copy of the transaction to the referee office. Table 3 shows the transaction characteristics including action times, multiplying **A** factors and the calculated points for each office.

Table 3

Office	Number of employees (NE)	Transaction category (CT)	Standard time of completing (ST) in minutes	Grace time (GT) in minutes	Action time (AT) in minutes	Multiplying factor (A)	Office points obtained from this transaction	Standard multiplying factor	Standard points
11	6	4	4	8	3	1.5	6	1	4
21	5	1	1	2	2	0	0	1	1
22	4	2	2	4	3	0.6	1.2	1	3
31	5	3	3	6	3	1	3	1	1
33	3	2	2	4	3	0.36	0.72	1	2

And of course, the multiplying **A** factor is evaluated according to packets which this transaction has been delivered with, in addition to procedures taken by the offices. And now there are many possibilities and I'm going to discuss a few of them:

First Case

Office 11 erred truly in treating the transaction. It passed through all offices without figuring out mistakes till it was revealed by office 33, which in turn found the mistake was done by office 11. Office 33 turned the mistaken transaction to office 11 and a copy to the referee office.

The referee office had confirmed existence of the error in 9 minutes (late for the grace time of 8 minutes), then the office 33 awards, the total earned points of the offices that have erred with the same transaction, ST_{total}

$$ST_{total} = \sum ST_{office} \qquad (16)$$

$ST_{total,\ office33} = 1 \times 4 + 1 \times 1 + 1 \times 3 + 1 \times 1 = 9$ points.

The earned $ST_{total,\ office33}$ for office 33 will be subtracted from the other offices, and the multiplying **A** factors will be subjected to equation 15 for these offices, as in Table 4.

Table 4

Office	Before the error was discovered			After the referee office has established the existence of the error; all offices bear this error except 33. Changes the multiplying **A** factors and the points for each office as follows			
	Multiplying A factor	Standard multiplying A factor	Standard points (ST)	Multiplying A factor	Points	Inverted standard points	Total points
11	1.5	1	4	0	0	--4	--4
21	0	1	1	-1	-1	-1	-2
22	0.6	1	3	0	0	--3	--3
31	1	1	1	0	0	-1	-1
33	0.36	1	2	0.36	0.72	+9	9.72

Also, the delay of referee office is subject to Haseeb system, as shown in Table 5.

Table 5

Office	Number of employees (NE)	Transaction category (CT)	Standard transaction time (ST), min.	Grace time (GT), min.	Action time (AT) min.	Office points from this transaction
Referee office	5	4	4	8	9	- 3.2

At the same time the transaction 519 will be returned within a packet to office 11 and start as a completely new transaction.

Second Case

All offices performed their work correctly but office 33 considered that office 11 erred in a procedure, and then, sent a copy of it to the referee office and returned the transaction to office 11.

Within 5 minutes, the referee office had found office 33 wrong. Then, the office 11 earns standard points on the expense of office 33 and the transaction is returned to office 33 as a new transaction, and the rest of the offices have no change in their points, Table 6. The referee office gained points as shown in Table 7.

Table 6

Office	Before return			After the referee office proves the error wasn't existed, the office 11 gains points in the expense of office 33. **A** factors and points are to be changed as follows			
	Multiplying **A** factor	Standard multiplying **A** factor	Standard points (**ST**)	Multiplying **A** factor	Points	Standard points (**ST**)	Total points
11	1.5	1	4	1.5	6	2+ (2)	10
21	0	1	1	0	0	-	0
22	0.6	1	3	0.6	1.2	-	1.2
31	1	1	1	1	3	-	3
33	0.36	1	2	0	0	-2	-2

Table 7

Office	Number of employees (**NE**)	Transaction category (**CT**)	Standard transaction time (**ST**), min.	Grace time (**GT**), min.	Action time (**AT**) min.	Office points from this transaction
Referee office	5	4	4	8	5	2.6

Haseeb system controls passing transactions from one office to another and rule the relationship between them and help them make the right decision and not pass the wrong transaction.

1.7 Stages of a Treatment

At the end of each financial month and for each completed transaction, Haseeb system evaluates the number of treating stages, R_o, by calculating the number of offices it had passed through, including the re-treatment progress.

Example (1-5)

If all stages in example 1-4 was done during the fiscal January, then:

Stages of treatment in the first case, $R_o = 10$; while $R_o = 7$ in the second case.

In the first case, we note that the re-treating phases of the returned transaction have been added as a claim was sent to the referee office and at the same time it returned to the office 11 and then passed on to the rest of the offices.

In the second case the re-treatment was added as a claim was sent to the referee office and the transaction was sent back to the office 33.

1.8 The Department

The management office of the department is treated as any of the other offices, and it gains fiscal monthly points, **DP**, from its offices equals to a rate of total office points divided by the stages where the transactions have gone through the offices of the department;

$$DP = \frac{r \sum_{i,month} MO_i}{RD} \qquad (17)$$

Where, **r**: is **the rate coefficient, MO: the fiscal monthly points of an office, RD: total stages passed during the department of all treated transactions in the department.**

The points of department management office are distributed over the management staff.

$$p_1 + p_2 + .. + p_n = 1 \qquad (18)$$

Where, p_1: **Department manager ratio**, p_2: **First deputy ratio,** and so on.

Example (1-6)

Let's suppose that a department includes the exampled office in example 1.1. The management office of this department includes a manager, a deputy and three employees, and the rate coefficient= **r** = 100.

The ratio of the manager and the deputy are 0.66 and 0.33, respectively.

Three sub-offices are included under this department: a, b and c. The total stages passed during the department of all treated transactions in the fiscal January=**RD**=700, and the monthly points, **MO**, of these offices are shown in Table 8.

Table 8

Office	Monthly points (MO)
a	2450
b	670
c	-100
Department management office	1100

The points of the department management office are divided as explained in the example (1-1), so that monthly gained points that gained by each of the deputy and three employees = **ME** = 0.8 × 1100/ 5 = 176 points.

While the manager get= **MM**= 0.2 x 1100 = 220 points, in addition to 176 points as a member of the office.

The management office gained monthly points from its sub-offices, **DP**= 100 × (2450 + 670-100)/ 700 = 431.42 points.

The manager and the deputy gained from it 284.74 and 142.37 points respectively.

We note that the Haseeb system rewards department management also for its role in the management of its affiliated offices and urges them to improve their performance. And so, the department will look for reasons for the underperformance of sub-office c to find a solution. It will also follow carefully the performance of staff and sub-office management, as well as the facilitation of transactional procedures, reducing the number of stages of transactions and thus increasing their points and, at the same time, reducing the time of completion of any transaction that the section reduces as far as possible between offices.

1.9 Foundation

At the end of each financial month, the total number of treated stages of all transactions passed through the organization's offices, **RO**, is calculated from:

$$RO = \sum_{o,month} R_o \qquad (19)$$

Where, R_o is the number of stages of a transaction through the organization, as described in examples 1-4 and 1-5.

The system also calculates the points score of offices that treat a transaction during the financial month, **POT**. Consequently, by summing all values of **POT** the monthly points of the organization from all transactions, **POM**:

$$POM = \sum_{t,month} POT_t \qquad (20)$$

Where **t**=1, 2,.. is treated transactions during the month.

Example (1-7)

A transaction was treated through a group of offices during fiscal October as in the following table:

Table 9

Office	Points the office obtained from this transaction
12	-4
25	3
31	2.5
32	-1.3
34	5

From the table:
Stages of treatment, R_o= 5
Points obtained by the offices from this transaction during the financial month, **POT**=-4 + 3 + 2.5-1.3 + 5 = 1.8

1.10 General Administration

Haseeb system treats the general administration differently

comparing to other institution's offices to avoid any kind of centralization of transactions and avoiding signing as many of them as possible to collect more points. As a result, the general administration is kept concerning on the supervision, management and fighting the accumulation of paper works.

Haseeb system rewards the general administration on the efficiency of treating the transactions by eliminating routine complications and saving time and effort. The more monthly the foundation points and reducing the number of stages of transactions and their completion time; the more increment of the efficiency of the institution. Also, there is no way to equate the comparison between two different institutions with the same number of points, but different in number of staff. Therefore Haseeb system also considers the number of employees of the organization as a performance measure.

At the end of each financial month, the general administration office gains points from the institution, **POG**:

$$POG = \frac{g \times POM}{RO \times NE_{institution}} \qquad (21)$$

Where: **g** is **the multiplying factor, POM: monthly points of the institution from all transactions, $NE_{institution}$: number of employees of the institution, RO: the total stages of all transactions that went through the institution's offices during the financial month.**

Example (1-8)

The monthly points of an institution from all transactions in fiscal November, **POM** = 120500 points, and the total stages of all transactions that went through the institution's offices, **RO**= 15020. If the number of employees, **$NE_{institution}$**=50, and the multiplying factor, **g** = 10000; then the points of general administration office, **POG** = 10000 ×120500/ (50 × 15020) = 1604.524 points.

In this case, the administration staff will focus on upgrading the performance of departments, offices and even employees, also it will be interested in reducing the number of stages of transactions as far as possible to accelerate the transaction and consequently increase the institution's monthly points.

The most efficient staff will be hired and rotated between offices to reduce the number of staff as much as possible to raise their share of points.

The points of general administration are divided to the general administrator, deputies and employees by predetermined proportions in the same manner described in example (1-6).

1.11 Vital Sections

Some sections and offices are considered vital for the institution, and its performance directly affects other departments. For example, offices cannot do tasks without stationery provided from the store which in turn gets it from a procurement office. If any of the store or procurement office is delayed in providing requirements quantity appropriate for other offices, so its dependent work entirely stops, and the multiplying **A** factors become negative.

In that case, the store or procurement office are charging the negative points after the decision of the referee office. In some cases, the procurement section may provide the store requirements at the appropriate time, but the latter was delayed in supplying the requirements and in this case the store is charged the negative points resulting from this delay. If the cause of the delay is beyond the control, the negative points are deducted from the institution's monthly points, so that it does not become an outlet for the cancelling of the negative points. The institution is required to find a solution for that delay such as dealing with another resource.

For convenience, electronic ordering is preferable to the requirements of the sections; if the administration department insists on centralizing the decision of needed distribution, the negative points are charged due to delay in approval to the central authority to make the decision.

1.12 Disbursement of the Financial Reward

One of the Haseeb committee tasks is determining the beginning and end of each transaction, and how to define the completion of a transaction, such as delivery to the customer, or delivered to the next institution or entity.

Haseeb system monitors the completion of each transaction, and then a financial reward derived from such completed transactions is calculated from the equation (13) in the final financial month in which it was finally completed.

Chapter 2 Mechanism of Haseeb System for Paper-Work

The first chapter focuses on the functioning idea of Haseeb system, in addition to some of its characteristics and relationships. But this chapter introduces the mechanism for using it in the departments that provide services based on paper documents, which are common in many institutions despite the use of computer networks and automated authentication.

2.1 Tools

The system in his simplest form needs to:

1- Haseeb boxes: Each of which is a closed box with a door, the upper face has a slot which suits entering the transaction papers and documents. Inside the box, a bar code reader is installed, Figure 2.

Each office has its own box, which is placed in a central location in the institution, accessible to all employees.

2- Alarms screen and speaker. Each office has its own alarming system installed in an appropriate place to notify all staff within the office. Also, they can see details of received transactions through the screen.

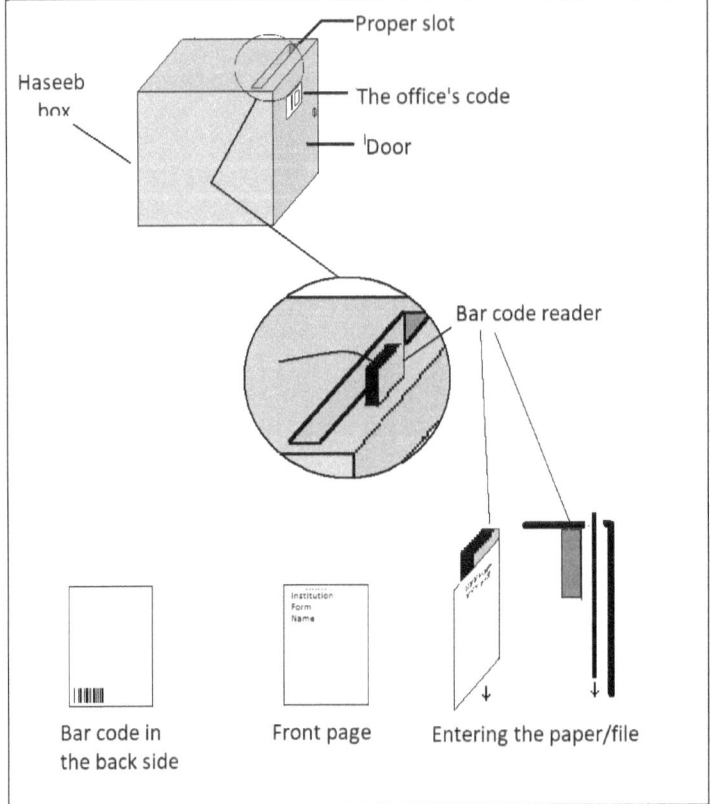

Figure 2: Haseeb box

3- A centralized computer monitors incoming and outcoming transactions for each office. The centralized computer organizes staff in offices according to their needs.
4- Transaction receiver: a computer records receiving of transactions and code them.
5- Transactional monitoring devices, which are peripheral devices in each office, the staff monitors the actions taken in respect of each transaction.
6- The staff presence monitor, within each office, has one or more devices, which identify the employees who are present during each working period.
7- Network between boxes, alarming systems, centralized computer and transaction receivers.

8- A system of communicating messages to clients, electronically connected to Haseeb system and one of the telecommunication networks provided for SMS services[5].

2.2 Classification of Foundation Offices

The offices of the institution are classified according to the mechanism of Haseeb system into:

1- Public Offices

They are the offices that deal with the public, customers or external clients. It is divided into:

Information office

It is responsible for responding to client's enquiries and handing out forms and paperwork for transactions, as well as for handing over their incomplete transactions for completion.

Transactional receiving office

It is competent to receive transactions from customers directly or indirectly through the receiving Haseeb box.

Delivery office

It is competent to hand over transactions that are ready for their owners.

2- Internal Offices

They are offices that do not receive clients or the public and receive transactions from other offices in the same institution.

---

[5] Nowadays, it is possible to use smart phone applications.

2.3 Mechanism of Dealing with Paper-Works

1- Outer Offices

Information offices

The public often complains about the long wait until they meet the information staff, get answers to their queries, or hand over their transactions.

To reduce waiting time, a lot of successful methods are used at many institutions. For example, guidance dashboards can be installed in the entrance to the customer lounge, numbering devices help in regulating the flow of customers on the reception windows while they can wait in comfortable chairs, some educational and promotional leaflets may be offered to kill waiting time. Many organizations have also successfully offered their services electronically on the phone or on the internet, and some have even been receiving transactions via the Internet, booking a transaction date and may be sent to the owner by mail[6].

Customer acceptance is different in getting answers to their queries through websites, automated telephone or guidance boards from someone to else; many of them are only persuaded by the direct answer of the information officer, which explains the congestion of the reception and information offices.

The Haseeb system accommodates all possible ways of information and reception of the public, pays attention to this section of the institutions and aims to transfer interest in the transaction from the client to the employee.

Self-query

A self-query, Figure 3, means the query through which the customer obtains answers to his enquiries without meeting the employees of the organization and can perform this in known ways such as dashboards,

---

[6] The smartphone applications were not introduced at the time of writing the book

automated telephone and web sites. A self-help query--round the clock--can respond to public inquiries, clarify all details about the papers and documents required, and the forms for each transaction and how to fill in the information, place of delivery, time of work and fees and payment methods, the following procedures and expected time to accomplish the transaction. The success of a self-help query depends on the organization's seriousness in providing these services to the public, updating it, training its staff, and spreading awareness among the public of the effectiveness of the self-inquiry. On the other hand, the public interacts with the self-query each according to his or her awareness, culture and experience. For a self-help inquiry to succeed, the institution must actively activate its role towards it and raise awareness among the public in how to use it, some institutions may make the best use of competent companies that provide this service.

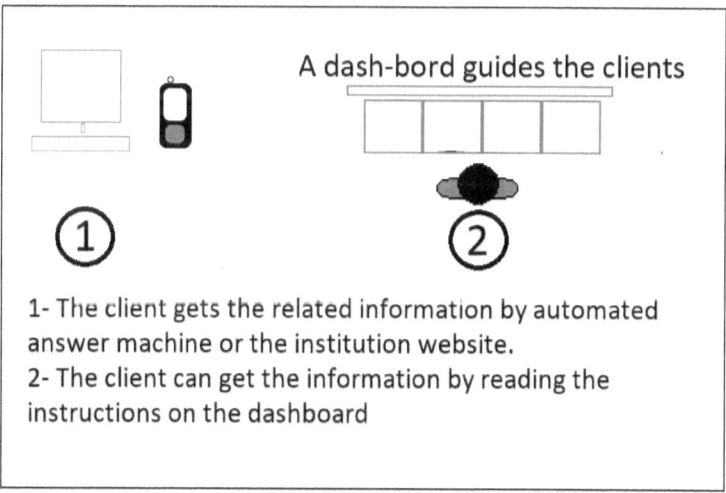

Figure 3: Self-query methods

Information desk

Haseeb system focuses on rewarding employees according to their effort, work, commitment and achievement. To invest this feature in information office, it connects the customer's fulfillment of its requirements and queries, and the employee who has performed this service efficiently. It also depends on the rotation of staff from the less crowded offices to the busiest, and in order to reach these objectives, some of the steps taken in the information office must be clarified.

Client guidance devices are placed in the entrance to the reception lounge and direct clients to places of service and at the same time regulate their flow to the information windows. Amenities are provided by lounge chairs, educational paintings, etc. This service we see in a lot of successful institutions.

Each information window is equipped with a transactional monitoring device, linked to the Haseeb system network. Also, the information window desk is provided with accompanying bulletins showing how to fill the required forms, sheets, and so on to facilitate the task of the information employee.

When the client enters, he goes to the client presence monitoring device and takes a receipt according to the type of service he/she is looking for. The voucher loads a number and shows the expected time for service delivery. The client shall be directed to the place where the service is provided either from the same monitoring device or through guidance panels. The client monitoring device alerts the information desk to the number of customers based on the type of service.

When the role reaches the client, it displays its voucher number on the screen and the window to which the service will be provided. Till this point, the said services are found in many institutions.

After the information employee completes serving the client, answer his enquiries, and hand over the forms of his treatment, take the receipt from him and pass it on to the receipt monitoring of Haseeb system.

Haseeb system counts the number of customers that each employee has served and adds to his points.

Haseeb system also monitors customer waiting time, and based on their number and the number of serving employees, it evaluates the performance of the information office and expect the average service time for clients in the waiting lounge and the new arrivals. If the expected average waiting time is higher than a specific value due to the increasing number of clients, it is required electronically from staff located in less busy offices to go to help and reduce the waiting time. If the waiting time is reduced because of a lack of clients, it directs staff to more busy offices and thus adapts the number of query staff depending on the number of customers based on the evaluation of the Haseeb system, and each employee will receive as many customers as possible and harvest more points.

Thus, we get rid of the longer waiting time for clients by adapting the staff to the number of reviewers, and by increasing staff interest in good performance and speed of delivery.

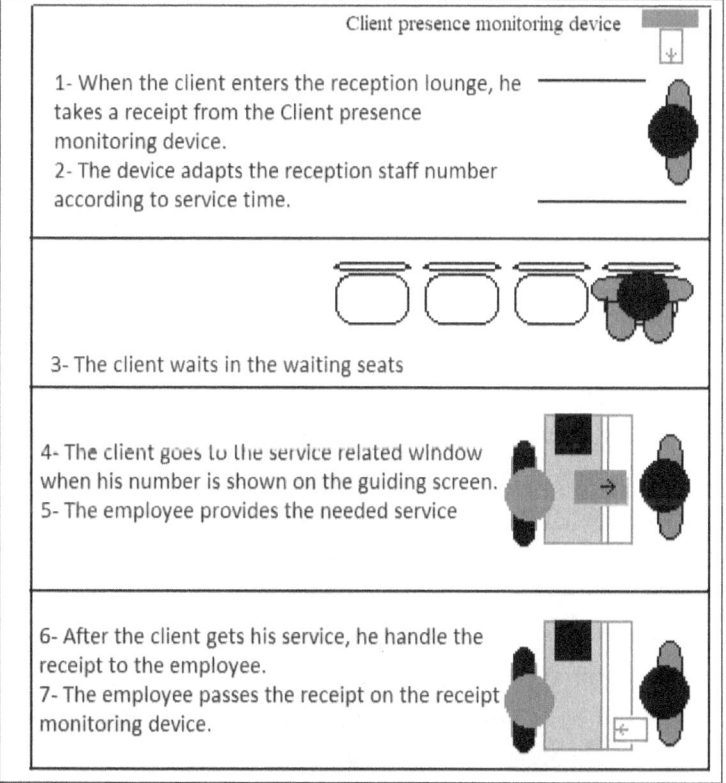

Figure 4: Dealing with the information desk

Transaction forms

Many successful organizations make it easier for their customers to access transaction forms through the internet or through electronic delivery devices or by providing them in private offices that are located around institutions. They also support clients in the methodology of filling the forms and the required documents. Also, they give examples on both the Internet and through the guide dashboards placed in the client entrance. In these ways the waiting time and errors are reduced, and the reception of transactions is accelerated. The clients can obtain whatever forms and inquiries are needed outside of the working hours and avoid the anticipated congestion in the information desk and directly handle ready forms to the transactional receiving office.

If special forms are to be received directly from the institution, they must be provided by the information desk. The private offices here can play their part in speeding up the process of selling and distributing forms.

Place on the forms the location of the customer's preferable contact methods: SMS, phone call, or he/she is going to review the delivery office himself.

Haseeb system adds bar code to each transaction form, which has the type of transaction and its category according to the organization's classification, plus a sequential number for the sheet. This code is readable through Haseeb box bar code reader.

If the transaction requires a set of papers and documents, the form can be a cartoon file and the code can be attached on its outer envelope, and the required papers are included inside.

Delivery of transactions

When a client completes preparation the form and attach the required documents within the encoded file "If the transaction contains a set of papers", he/she can deliver the transaction to the institution in two ways:

1- Put it in the recipient box.
2- Deliver directly to the receptionist.

Transactions recipient office

After the customer has met his treatment requirements and places it in a Haseeb recipient box, he/she can get a confirmation receipt. Haseeb system separates the transaction recipient office from the information office.

If the transaction contains important papers and documents, it can be delivered to the transaction receptionist and after the employee has ascertained that the papers and documents have been completed; the customer delivers a receipt confirming the transaction's deposit, this employee service is subject to Haseeb system.

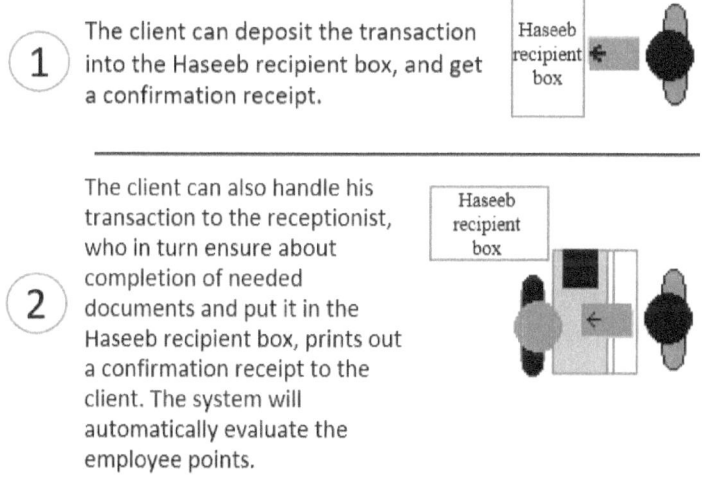

1. The client can deposit the transaction into the Haseeb recipient box, and get a confirmation receipt.

2. The client can also handle his transaction to the receptionist, who in turn ensure about completion of needed documents and put it in the Haseeb recipient box, prints out a confirmation receipt to the client. The system will automatically evaluate the employee points.

Figure 5: Depositing the transaction

When the staff receive the transaction, they will enter its data and encode each one, so that the given code is a companion to this transaction in each stage.

Haseeb system monitors the number of registered transactions made by the data entry and counts the points as described in Chapter 1.

In case of ability to serve, receive, review, treat and deliver transactions to the client, it is preferred to merge transaction reception with the information department.

Haseeb recipient box

A recipient committee can be formed to get transactions from Haseeb recipient boxes and may be separated as a department belong to the transaction recipient office.

Haseeb recipient box can read the encoding transaction and the deposit time and issues a preliminary notice for the client by receiving the transaction, and the related employee/department is alerted too.

If there is a transaction fee which could not be added to the form cost, Haseeb recipient box can be connected to an electronic cash receipt device, or an ATM to read credit card. The recipient committee must care about serving the box and get incentives to ensure the safety and continuity of its work.

Using this method, a client can deposit the transaction 24 hours a day throughout the year, avoiding waiting in lines or leaving the work.

At the beginning of each period, the box is opened. The transactions are checked and directed into the related box. For example, when the transaction form 125 ready, it is deposited in the box of the office A; and so on. Consequently, the client is notified about the procedure.

Haseeb system monitors the process and the office A reaction which has to receive it at the beginning of the period.

Incomplete transactions are transferred to enterprise queries; the customer reports a lack of information or documents.

Verification of the completeness of the papers and documents is the responsibility of the recipient office. When an incomplete transaction is transferred to the next destination, the transaction is returned to the recipient office and a copy is sent to the referee office, as mentioned in Chapter 1.

2- Internal Offices

Reviewing of clients to the internal offices must be reduced as much as possible. Using Haseeb system, the transaction is followed up and the time lost in the archives office or the indicative figures for inbound and outbound are eliminated.

Any lack of transaction documents also requires transferring it directly to the information office and reporting the client, thereby eliminating the flow of clients into the institution, search for theirs, contact employees, looking for solutions to overcome the defects of the transaction, etc.

Let's take an example of following a transaction form 716.

The said transaction was placed in the Haseeb recipient box, the system monitors the transaction and exits it from the custody of the recipient office to the custody of the next related office, A.

At the beginning of the following period, a staff member from the office A received the said transaction included in a transactions packet.

Having completed the necessary treatment, a staff member shall record the action taken regarding the transaction in the transaction monitor system.

And then, it shall be placed in the following office box, office B, for the next procedure.

The transaction continues to be passed from one office to another until the transaction is finalized in office 11 and deposited with the delivery office box.

The system monitors the exit of the transaction 716 from the custody of office 11 and enters the custody of the delivery office and informs the client of its readiness and ability to receive it.

When the delivery office receives the transactions, it sorts the transactions according to the delivery method to the customer, by mail or hand-delivered.

When the client arrives to receive the transaction by hand, the employee takes the receipt and give the completed transaction to the client.

The Haseeb system evaluates the total working time to complete each transaction and monitors the delay and the management can address each problem and find solutions that increase the quality of the services provided by the organization.

And so, from this part, we find that the Haseeb system has a range of advantages, most importantly:

- Reducing friction between clients and employees. By connecting a Web-based Haseeb system, the client can trace the treatment procedure without access to the institution, search for staff to assist, and the consequent occupancy of staff, wasting their time in receiving guests, visitors, etc.
- The time lost in each office is killed by the process of establishing the ref number and explaining the transaction, once the transaction has passed through the construction of a Haseeb box, the reader monitors the transaction depositing time, and the employees will only record the taken action in the program.

2.4 Haseeb Electronic System

The electronic system is different from the paper-work system, because the transactions are received electronically, through the telephone, the internet or a terminal computer network. The said receiving methods are connected to the institution system, and the client's response requires that some employees review some records, i.e. there is a human effort accompanies the completion of the transaction.

In this case we can dispense with Haseeb recipient boxes, and each office or employee has a party, monitors the receipt of the transaction and answers the transaction and sends to the next, the system monitors the working time for each transaction, in the same manner as in Chapter 1.

2.5 Mainstreaming Haseeb System

With some modifications, Haseeb system can be used in laboratories, hospitals, customs, universities, schools and all service institutions.

References

- متطلبات الحكومة الإلكترونية الفاعلة والعقبات التي تواجهها، محمود بن ناصر الريامي
http://www.araburban.org/egov/arabic/speakers.htm
- الفساد، أشكاله، أسبابه ودوافعه، وآثاره، ومكافحته واستراتيجيات الحد من تناميه، ومعالجته، زياد عربية ابن علي
http://www.malazi.com/index.php?d=95&id=33
- التأخر عن العمل وعدم إتقانه، منور بن عمر الحربي
http://www.moj.gov.sa/website1/result.aspx?id=9
- مقالات في الإدارة، الحوافز... إدارة الأفراد
http://www.quran-radio.com/edara3.htm
- الرشوة خلل كبير في الواجب الوظيفي، عبد الله بن راشد السنيدي
http://www.al-jazirah.com.sa/2007jaz/feb/9/ar2.htm
- الفساد في العالم العربي، نبيل علي صالح
http://www.dctcrs.org/s3818.htm
- الأردن والجزائر نموذجان، الفساد في العالم العربي متمأسس ومتمكن، إبراهيم علي غرايبة
http://www.aljazeera.net/NR/exeres/D9407C87-442D-41C9-9F68-1C7E21D11AE2.htm
- النزاهة ومتلازمة الفساد والفقر والإرهاب، الجزء الأول، فارس حامد عبد الكريم
http://www.annabaa.org/nbancws/70/163.htm

- مفاهيم القرآن
http://www.rafed.net/books/olom-quran/mafahim-al-quran-6/18.html

- مصطلحات القرآن
http://www.koothta.com/islam/dar_alquran/details.asp@id=675.htm

www.ingramcontent.com/pod-product-compliance
Lightning Source LLC
Chambersburg PA
CBHW030510220526
45464CB00006B/2734